MW01643833

Mark Harris

RIDING THE WAVE OF LIFE

RIDING THE WAVE OF LIFE

Cover photo: My son Willie Harris; pondering the waves of Maui.

I dedicate this book to my adorable children

Whitney and Willie

Prologue

Surfing and the game of life are the perfect metaphors to describe the adventure of being alive.

As I sit on my surfboard staring out to the horizon, I am struck on how much surfing parallels with being alive.

As I patiently wait for the next wave to arrive, this reminds me of how we wait patiently for our next opportunity to arrive.

As the wave approaches the excitement starts to build, much like the feeling you get when you are approaching a new life challenge.

You paddle so hard to catch the wave, working like there will never be another wave.

When your life opportunity presents itself, your hard work to grab that opportunity comes into play.

As a surfer, you know when you have enough momentum and you catch the wave. The exhilaration, the accomplishment, and the pure joy of riding the wave, now that is what surfing is all about.

Landing the job of your dreams, landing the relationship of your dreams, fulfilling your life's purpose is much like riding the wave of life.

As much as you don't want the ride to end, the wave dwindles or sometimes a mistake is made, and you come crashing down.

Life is much like that, even though we want to stay on top, we never do. The only for sure thing in this life is, it is always changing.

We are either getting on a wave or falling off a wave. Our career is either moving up or it may be moving down. Same with relationships, they are either growing stronger or they are slowly diminishing.

This is my story, this is my journey through life, the successes and the failures, the ups and the downs. This truly is my story of riding the wave of LIFE!

Chapter 1

Little league

Self-confidence, are we born with it? Does it come from our early years? Did our parents enhance the confidence? All questions I have pondered over the years, this is my journey to answer these questions.

My first real memory as a little boy of 6 years old, the first day of little league baseball practice. I was so excited I barely slept the night before. A real baseball team, and I was going to get a real hat and a t-shirt I had longed for.

I woke up, I ate breakfast and rode my bike to practice. Meeting the coach, showing my skill as a ball player, all a 6-year old's dream.

After practice walking into the kitchen my mom asks, "How was practice?" Not missing a beat, I blurt out "I'm the best one on the team!"

Was I the best one on the team? Probably not, but the point is, I thought I was.

This is my story or my journey through life. From 6 to 60, all riding the wave of life.

I'll take you on a journey from growing up in a small farming community in Iowa to working the ultimate dream job on a cruise ship in Alaska, Hawaii and Antarctica.

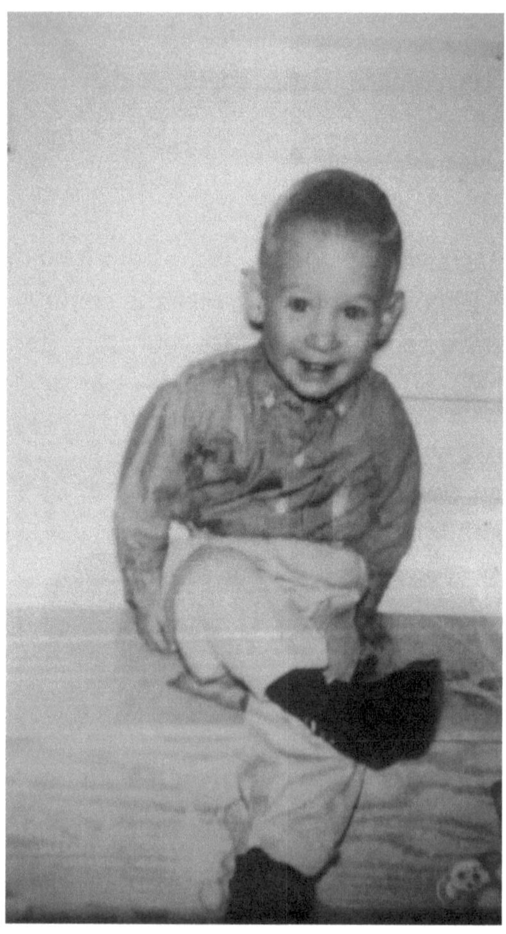

Mark Harris (age 4)

Lessons learned at a young age tend to shape and mold us as adults. My mother was not only a good mother but a great teacher.

When I was 12 years old I joined the swim team in my small town of Algona, Iowa. Now Algona, Iowa is not the swimming capital of the world, just a small community with a lot of pride.

My first day of practice was brutal. I thought I could swim but after practice I was so exhausted I had no idea how I was going to get home. There were 2 giant hills I had to climb to get home. Looking back the hills were small, but I was very tired.

I walked into the house, put my towel and swimsuit down and defiantly told my mother "I'm quitting". Boy, was that the wrong thing to say to my mother.

For the next 30 minutes she made it perfectly clear that when you start something you do not have the option to quit.

She would allow me not to join next year but since I had started the season, it was not an option to quit. I will finish the season no matter what and that was the final word, no discussion.

I did finish the season, won a few of the local meets and all in all had a great time.

The final state meet had come. The winners received trophies, I dreamt of winning the trophy for the 50-meter breaststroke.

I cleared a place on my shelf in the bedroom, I envisioned the trophy sitting there after I would win the event.

The day came, a warm summer day in Jefferson, Iowa. I climb onto the starting blocks, the pool is only 25 meters long, so I must go across and back with one turn.

The gun sounds, I am off chasing the gold. I think I am swimming so fast, the gold is mine, but no.

As I turn to swim the last length of the pool I look up and my competitors all have finished. They are climbing out of the pool and I still have 25 more meters to go.

Wow, that was a swim of shame. I climbed out dejected, my dreams slashed but my friends Paul Martin and Randy Nielsen were laughing so hard I had to laugh with them.

To this day I still get a little ribbing for being so slow, but what a memory. So was I a good swimmer, no way, but I do thank my mother for making me finish the season.

Another life changing lesson came from my mother. Commitment was the lesson and friendship was the factor.

I was friends with a neighbor boy named Mike Diamond. We had been neighbors since I was 4 years old. Mike called and invited me over to his house to play as children do.

On my way out the phone rings, Ricky Petersen calls and invites me to come over. Well Ricky had some cool toys to play with and Mike didn't have much to offer, so without hesitation I told Ricky I'll be over.

My mother heard the conversation, sat me down and with no uncertainty gave me a severe tongue lashing.

The bottom line is when you make a commitment you follow through, no matter what the consequences are. Even if you have a chance to upgrade, once a commitment is made the upgrade is not an option.

This lesson has made my life so simple and really rewarding. Do I get offers to upgrade once I have made a commitment, sure we all do?

But when you live by this one principle alone and honor your first commitment, life just seems to fall into place in the natural order.

There is one motto my mother ingrained in me, “Say what you mean, and mean what you say.”

Can you fail and laugh at the same time? Yes, that is what is so much fun about living this life.

Even now as old as I am, I still see Paul and Randy laughing as I climb out of the pool. Failure is not fatal, just something that happens when you try.

The key to overcoming failure is believing and believing is the common denominator all great people have. To believe and not be afraid of failure is what living is all about.

Chapter 2

The Village

"It takes a village to raise a child" these words ring true to my life. My small farming community set a course for my life and the journey has been incredible. Idols and mentors, this really is what shapes us all.

Dave Martin, my first idol, and now a very close friend. Dave was a high school wrestler, football player, and baseball catcher. The three sports that I followed reverently as an 8-year-old boy.

I watched Dave win the state championship as a wrestler, I watched him receive an all-state football selection, and an all-conference baseball award. He was my idol, I loved sports and I was determined to pattern my life after Dave.

Call it intervention, call it coincidence, the Martin family moved into my neighborhood. My sports idol just a few houses away. Dave's sister Linda had been my favorite babysitter. Linda was my babysitter of choice, when she babysat I would continually ask her questions about her brother.

Dave signed his letter of intent to wrestle for Iowa State University and off to college he went. Champ Martin, the father of the Martin family and the high school wrestling coach.

If there ever was a man among men, Champ Martin was that kind of man. Quiet, strong, and loving, all qualities of a great man.

When Champ Martin entered a room the whole aura changed, you realized you were in the presence of someone special.

His wife Dottie loved life more than anyone I have ever met. A strong committed Christian woman with a heart of gold. She admired her children and she is one woman that glowed.

The best thing about the Martin family moving into my neighborhood was the 2 youngest boys. Paul Martin is 1 year older than I am and Jim Martin, 1 year younger than me.

Paul and I became inseparable friends, paper routes, county fairs, fishing, camping and bike riding, all what little boys in Iowa do.

Bill Manske, the epitome of a loving father was another incredible role model in my life. I was 13 years old and I received a phone call, on the other end was Bill.

He began to explain the situation; his son Ron was my age and new to Algona. Ron was having an extremely hard time adjusting to a move from Blue Earth, Minnesota to Algona, Iowa.

Ron was a star golfer, in Blue Earth, Minnesota, he could have played on the varsity golf team as an eighth- grader but in Algona he would have to wait until his freshman year to play varsity golf.

Ron was so upset with the move he refused to go to school. Bill swallowed all his pride, somehow found my phone number and out of the blue asked, maybe pleaded a little for me to be Ron's friend.

Ron Manske and I became best friends, all because a loving father took the time to reach out to a total stranger.

I could have said no but I would have missed out on two of the most precious relationships I have had in this lifetime.

In the summer I worked for Bill in the field drainage business. We laid drainage tile in Iowa and Minnesota corn fields.

At that time Bill had 3 boys all around my age that could have worked for him. His giving and loving nature for his boys was so apparent.

Hiring me, his boys had the freedom to pursue their dreams. All his boys were tremendous golfers and during the summer the time was used for them to perfect their skill.

Only a loving and caring father would put his children's dreams ahead of his own. This example molded me as a young man. Bill Manske was another man among men.

I entered my eighth-grade year, my history teacher was Dale Bahr. Wow, I was in heaven, Dale was a national wrestling champion from Iowa State University and now he was my history teacher.

Dale Bahr came to Algona, Iowa as the head wrestling coach. Champ Martin had been the Algona High School wrestling coach for many years and was retiring from the sport of wrestling.

By this time in my life I knew I not only wanted to be a state wrestling champion, but I wanted to be a national wrestling champion.

This same year, I watched my idol Dave Martin become a national wrestling champion at Iowa State University and a bonus, the Iowa State team also took home the title.

Dale became my coach, my mentor, and most of all my friend. We fished, we camped, we hung out and when the sun went down at night, I knew someone really cared about me. Allow me to share my favorite Dale Bahr story.

My freshman year in high school I made the varsity wrestling team. Granted, I was not that good, but as luck would have it the senior wrestler in my weight class was forced to sit out the season with chronic knee problems.

Terry Alt was the senior wrestler, and his season ended abruptly. This put me in a precarious spot. I was overjoyed to make the varsity team but on the other hand I was not prepared for the pressure of being a varsity wrestler.

The first dual meet of the season was an away meet in Spencer, Iowa. Coach Bahr had done the math and figured my match would be the key match of either winning or losing the dual meet.

Coach had asked Terry to come along and weigh in just in case the meet was too close. Coach Bahr felt more confident going with a senior rather than trust a freshman like me.

As the meet unfolded, sure enough it came down to me. If I win, the team wins, if I lose, we lose the dual meet.

I'm nervous, I'm scared, but I am ready. Then at the last moment Coach Bahr yells at Terry to get his uniform on.

Granted, Terry is in the stands just watching the meet with his banged-up knees. He jumps down, runs to the locker room and puts his wrestling singlet on.

Now I am really confused, would Coach Bahr really put Terry out there and leave me on the sidelines.

He is my friend, my mentor, my coach, he must believe in me. There is no way he would do that to me, I love this man and I really believe he loves me.

Then, the toughest words to hear "Terry, go win this meet". Wow, my heart ripped out, my spirit torn, dejected I sink into the chair on the edge of the mat.

I watch as Terry destroys his opponent and becomes the hero of the night. My world is spinning, I feel horrible, my stomach is turning over. I get queasy, I don't want to cry but can't really help it, the tears start to stream down my face.

Coach Bahr makes his way over to me, I look up and tears are streaming down his face. He cups my face with his loving hands, no words are exchanged, and he hugs me. Not an ordinary hug, but a genuine I love you hug.

At that moment I knew he was hurting as much as I was, and the world was righted.

We all have moments that define us as human beings, this was a defining moment.

I not only learned decisions are tough to make but sometimes decisions hurt and hurt bad. But a decision made with love; is what life is all about.

With Coach Bahr, I went on to have a great wrestling career, even to the point of placing 2nd in the United States National Freestyle Wrestling Tournament.

I call this story "The Handshake", ever have a moment in time where time seems to stop? My senior year of high school started out with a little uncertainty.

My wrestling coach, Dale Bahr left Algona to be the assistant wrestling coach at Iowa State University. As fate would have it, Champ Martin was asked to coach 1 more year. Coming out of retirement, Champ took over the reins and was grooming Bill Fjetland for the head coaching job. Now that is turning a lemon into lemonade.

Having the chance to wrestle for a legend, is a dream come true. For the past 3 years I was conditioned before stepping on the mat to wrestle I had always shook Coach Bahr's hand for good luck. When the match was over, and I walked back to the bench I was always greeted with a handshake whether I had won or lost.

The wrestling season just began, the first match with Coach Martin. It was my turn to go out and compete, as I go I put out my hand for my good luck handshake. Champ Martin looks at me, shakes his head no.

Bewildered, I look at him like what is going on? He smiles and says, "I'll shake your hand when you win the state and I'll give you your medal".

It was a tradition in Iowa High School Wrestling that the coach of the state champion gives the medals to all the state placers on the victory stand.

30 times I went out to compete without a handshake, just a smile. 30 times I was victorious and came off the mat with just a smile.

My final match in the state tournament, I did win easily, but the whole last 2 minutes all I could think about was being able to shake Coach Martin's hand.

When I stood on top of the victory stand, my smile was so huge, I finally will get to shake Champ Martin's hand. My heart was racing as I watched him hand out the medals to the other placers.

He comes to me, this is when time stopped. He pauses, looks up, smiles and extends his hand. I clutch his hand and all I feel is pure, genuine love pulsate through my soul. I can hear the crowd cheering, but just barely.

This moment in time is so precious, our eyes meet and at this small space in time, my life is defined. To this day whenever a hand is extended, I grasp that hand with the same love and attention Champ Martin extended to me.

Looking back, that single handshake molded my life. Riding the wave of life started with a single handshake, I now knew anything in this life was possible.

In my case it did take a village to raise a child. These strong role models came into my life and gave me the greatest gift of all - their time.

I'm not afraid to say I love these men, they loved me first. My role models, my mentors all had one thing in common.

Relationships far outweigh anything else in life. Jobs, careers, commitments are all trivial to a real and genuine relationship.

Shaking Coach Champ Martin's hand (age 18)

Chapter 3

College

When you are 18 years old and faced with a life altering decision, life can seem to overwhelm you.

I did receive a lot of attention from college coaches after placing second in the National High School Freestyle Wrestling Tournament. I also then went on to win the Iowa State High School Championship in my weight class.

Recruiting trips started to pour in, college coaches were coming to my high school to see me. I was feeling like a celebrity in my small farming community.

Paul Martin, my best friend, he had signed his letter of intent to wrestle at Oklahoma State University where his brother Dave, my sports idol, was the assistant coach.

I really wanted to go to Oklahoma State at the time, but the boy who had beaten me in the national tournament finals was at Oklahoma State making it not possible for me.

Many schools thought it was a given that I would sign with Iowa State University since my high school coach, Dale Bahr, was the assistant at Iowa State.

Then along comes Bob Carlson from Utah State University. Bob was charismatic, flamboyant, and eccentric. I did visit the University of Northern Iowa, I took my visit to Iowa State and then decided to take one last visit to Utah State University.

I fly into Salt Lake City, surrounded by beautiful mountains and Coach Carlson picks us up. I was with Don Erickson; his brother Bob was already wrestling at Utah State.

On our way to Logan which is 75 miles north of Salt Lake City, Coach Carlson remarks "we have a lot of LDS people in Utah". I look over to my friend Don and whispered, "does he mean hippies?" I figured he just mixed up the letters.

Coach Carlson laughs and goes on to explain LDS is Latter Day Saints or Mormons. I look at Don and ask, "What is a Mormon?"

Well, after the recruiting trip to Utah I knew what a Mormon was, I was like fresh meat for the return missionaries.

I return home and am faced with a major decision, Utah State or Iowa State, what do I do. I grabbed some paper, listed the pros and cons, and it was apparent Utah State was where I wanted to be.

I was choosing to be a big fish in a small pond. I was giving up my dream of being a national champion, the caliber of the wrestling room and the competition was not nearly what

Iowa State had to offer. But the opportunities seemed endless in Utah.

Hiking, fishing, camping, rafting, just a plethora of opportunities besides wrestling. I signed my national letter of intent to wrestle for Utah State University.

Eight of the ten spots on my college wrestling team were guys from north central Iowa so I did feel somewhat at home.

Telling Coach Bahr at Iowa State that I was not coming was one of the toughest phone calls I have ever made. He was like a father to me and now I was abandoning him, leaving the state for Utah, a hard pill for him to swallow.

After the call, I was feeling horrible and the phone rings. On the other end was Nancy Bahr, Dale's wife, assuring me I made the right decision. She told me how proud she was of me and that Dale also was very proud. She explained he was a little hurt, but he will come around.

She ended by saying they both loved me. Many times, in my life, the minute I feel the ship is going under, new life is breathed into me. Why is it in your darkest hou,r it is also your brightest hour?

Joe Sindelar and I grew up together, only 4 houses apart. Joe was 1 year older than me, but he had a sister my age. Often, I would use his sister as way to get into his house and play with his toys.

Joe and I were competitive when it came to neighborhood games. As we grew up, we grew apart until one night, and that night did change our lives.

I had taken all my recruiting trips and it was decision time. I traveled down to Ames, Iowa the home of Iowa State University to see a girl I had met on my recruiting trip.

I was at a party and realized I had no place to sleep that night. I had my sleeping bag with me, knowing I had quite a few friends that attended Iowa State.

Like any true blooded male, I was hoping to meet up with the girl had I traveled to see. Never happened, and now I am scrambling.

I run into Joe, he is a freshman at Iowa State and quickly ask "mind if I crash on your dorm room floor?" No problem was his reply.

That night I throw out my sleeping bag, thinking Joe is already asleep, I lie down. In the darkness Joe asks, "where are you going to sign?" I explain my decision to attend Utah State.

Out of the blue Joe blurts out "can I go with you?" We were not very close, so the response stunned me. Joe explains his plan to leave Iowa State, come with me and wrestle for Utah State.

I chuckle, and candidly say "Joe, you are not any good, what makes you think you can wrestle in college when you didn't even make our high school team?"

Didn't faze him at all, when I packed the car to go to Utah State, Joe came with me.

He worked so hard, not only did he make a NCAA division 1 wrestling team but was a 2-time conference champion while at USU.

Any time I started to feel sorry for myself I would look at Joe, what he overcame to be successful was nothing short of remarkable.

Watching Joe strike out into unknown territory with just a dream and then accomplishing it, gave me the confidence to begin riding the wave of life!

High School graduation (age 18)

I wrestled 4 years for Utah State in the 167-pound weight class. I had a great career, but as in life there is always irony. My senior year going into the national tournament I was seeded eighth in my weight class and Mark Churella from the University of Michigan was seeded first. Being seeded that way meant, if we both won our two preliminary rounds we would meet in the quarterfinals.

Mark Churella was already a 2-time national champion going for his third title, but the ironic part was Dale Bahr, my high school coach, was now his coach at the University of Michigan.

Going into the match I was feeling very confident, the previous day I had pinned my two preliminary opponents and I noticed Mark had struggled with his first two opponents.

Thinking I have a chance, I shake hands and the match begins. I have Coach Carlson, my coach yelling but I am also tuned into my old high school coach, Dale Bahr yelling. The man that taught me how to wrestle is now coaching my opponent.

Life will twist in an odd way at times and this is one twist hard to explain. As the match progressed, Keith Young, was the referee.

Keith was from my hometown, Algona. He was a former national champion at the University of Northern Iowa.

The third and final period rolled around, and I noticed the score. The scoreboard was reading 2 to 1, but the 2 was flashing. I asked Keith what the score really was.

He smiled and said, "when the score goes over 20, it just flashes". Oh wow, 22 to 1, now that is a drubbing. In today's sport of wrestling there is now a mercy rule, once you are ahead by 15 points the match is over.

Mark went on to win his third title and Dale Bahr continued to become a legend at the University of Michigan.

My years at Utah State University gave me countless friendships, treasured memories, and defining moments as a man. I had successes, I had failures, but more importantly I had fun.

1976

Chapter 4

Oklahoma

"The world is your oyster", what does that really mean? You hear that phrase a lot when you graduate from an institution. I always interpreted that phrase as the world is going to surround you with crap and it's up to you, to turn that crap into a pearl.

Graduating and heading out into the world, my next step. I was flat out broke, I left Logan, Utah and Utah State University with a degree in my pocket and barely enough money to get home back to Iowa. I pull into Algona, Iowa and there is Joe Sindelar waiting for me.

New Year's Eve in Iowa is not where I wanted to be. Cold, lonely, and miserable are the only adjectives I can use to describe how I was feeling. I was working on the Bjustrom hog farm to make a little money.

I have a teaching degree in my pocket with really no job prospects until the next school year. The ball is dropping in

New York City, midnight there but in Algona it's only 10 o'clock in Iowa.

After the ball drops the news comes on, I look at Joe and say, "let's move to the city that is the warmest." We both chuckle, but I am dead serious.

As the cities across the US scroll down with the temperatures, Phoenix wins with a temperature of 78 degrees.

The very next day Joe and I buy our plane tickets to Phoenix. Off to Phoenix we go, I pack my 10-speed bicycle into a box, grab a duffle bag of clothes and board the plane.

We have a friend in Phoenix that I call to pick us up at the airport. Dawn Erickson meets us as we arrive in Phoenix. Seeing her smile and the warm weather was refreshing.

Dawn had a 2-bedroom apartment in Tempe. The night before we arrived, her roommate had eloped and moved out without telling Dawn. She was in a quandary, wondering how she could afford the rent. Well, Joe and I needed a place to live and we all quickly agreed, this is it.

I had a little money saved and Joe had a little money saved so we were not in a hurry for a job. There was a pool at the complex, tennis courts at the Arizona State campus and beautiful sun kissed girls all around. We were in paradise. Our day consisted of playing tennis in the morning and lounging by the pool in the afternoon.

One morning in the middle of January the phone rings. It's Paul Martin, after Paul finished competing he became the assistant wrestling coach at Oklahoma State University.

I asked Paul how he found this phone number. He explained making a call to my mother to figure out where I was.

"There is a job for you here in Oklahoma", what had happened was the high school wrestling coach in Cushing, Oklahoma had just been fired for having an affair with a high school cheerleader. Cushing High School needed a wrestling coach and they needed one now.

There were two problems, the first one was I really didn't want to go. I was having so much fun playing tennis, swimming and enjoying the sun of Arizona I really had no interest in going to Oklahoma.

The second problem was, if I spent the money for a plane ticket to Oklahoma that would exhaust my money. My rent was paid, life was good, so I told Paul "no thanks".

Telling Paul Martin no, was in hindsight, a mistake. Paul is probably the top personal injury lawyer in the United States. He is one that knows how to argue, negotiate, and twist any outcome his way. I didn't stand a chance, and when I hung up the phone, I was on my way to Oklahoma.

Paul had a personal interest in me taking this job, his brother-in-law, Ricky Ahrberg, was a senior in high school and was on the team. This team was desperate for a coach and I guess it was me. I boxed up my bike, packed my clothes, said good-bye to Joe and off to Oklahoma I go.

Chapter 5

Teaching World

My first teaching job, Cushing High School started out strange to say the least. I graduated with a double major, Biology and Physical Education with a Health minor.

Arriving in Cushing, Oklahoma in the middle of winter is not what you call paradise. I just left Tempe, Arizona with the warm sun and stunning scenery. Cushing was a far cry from warm and the scenery was non-existent. What was I thinking?

Dr. Purcell was the principal at Cushing High School, I was face to face with him. He started to interview me as if I were applying for the job.

After a while I couldn't take the interview questions and stopped the interview abruptly. "Why are we going with this charade, I know I am your only choice and I just spent my last dollar to get here so let's just skip this part and tell me where the wrestling room is".

He was taken a back, he tried to recover but I wouldn't back down. I had just given up a great time in Tempe to come to Cushing. I figured he owed me the job for just showing up. Call it confidence, call it boldness, call it arrogance, or maybe call it stupidity, but I made it clear I was not going to play the interview game.

There was a long pause, we both were staring each other down. I had challenged his authority, I knew he wanted to retaliate but his back was against the wall. He needed a teacher and a coach, and he needed one today.

"OK the job is yours, can you start today?" No problem, I was the new Cushing High School head wrestling coach. My teaching assignment was next.

Dr. Purcell explained I was going to teach 2 coed physical education classes and 2 driver education/ health classes. I knew I could handle the PE classes and the health sections but had no clue how to teach driver education.

As we walked into the gym, he introduced me to 2 beautiful women that were my age. "These are your student teachers, they have been teaching your classes and you will be evaluating them".

No way, I am supervising student teachers, not only student teachers but hot student teachers. A huge smile creeps across my face, this is going to be fun.

I remember one afternoon the Oklahoma State University supervising instructor came to evaluate my student teachers. Sitting in the bleachers he asked, "how are they doing?" I replied with a smile "how should I know, I have never taught a day in my life."

What an awkward situation to be in, sometimes you just must chuckle, because when life gets goofy, you just must ride it out. They both got stellar evaluations from me. Looking back, that situation was so wrong on so many fronts.

I was staying with Dave Martin in Stillwater which is 24 miles from Cushing. I was using his car for the first few days but knew that wasn't going to work.

I took my bike out of the box, put it together. I would make the 2-hour ride to Cushing. Morning and night, the ride was starting to wear on me.

My student teachers taught my morning classes, so I took my time getting to school. One morning I pulled in around 10 o'clock looked in the gym, figured Jennifer had everything under control so I went into the locker room, filled the whirlpool tub, got naked and slipped into the tub. Soaking in the tub letting the world pass by and then, bam the gym door flies open and Jennifer runs in. She screams, "There is a fight, what am I supposed to do?"

Well Jennifer sees I am buck naked, blushes and realizes there is nothing I can do in the state I am in. I sometimes wonder what happened to my student teachers, now that was a wild ride.

My first day of wrestling practice. The coach had just been fired the week before. I had heard bits and pieces of the scandal but really didn't pay that much attention. The truth is hard to get to in situations like that because there is so much emotion involved.

I knew I was hired to do a job and I walked into that wrestling room to do it. Whoa, only 2 wrestlers were at practice. I was told there were 35 wrestlers on the team and now only 2 were in the room.

Ricky Ahrberg, which was Paul Martin's brother-in-law, and Paul Olsen. Both were seniors, I said "you two are the team?"

The whole team had quit in protest of the school firing their beloved coach. I shrugged and told them" I'm glad you are here, let's practice".

After practice, Ricky came over to me and said "Coach, I'll get the team back, don't worry". Sure enough all 35 wrestlers were back the next day.

We finished the year, both Ricky and Paul ended up being state placers. We came so close in upsetting the wrestling powerhouse, Perry, Oklahoma in a dual meet. The match came down to the heavyweight match, even though my wrestler was outmanned he fought his heart out.

The following year I moved to Cushing, coached freshman football, wrestling and tennis. I was teaching my own classes, life was good.

My salary was good, probably had more money than I knew what to do with. I bought a Volkswagen van, it was nice to have a vehicle to sleep in whenever I couldn't' get home.

So, after a few months I moved back to Stillwater, I enjoyed the college town. About mid-year I started to wonder, is this all there is to life?

I am single, and I was spending a great deal of time being an adult. I wasn't ready to be responsible, I wanted to play, not work. I found myself so tied up with no freedom.

After the high school wrestling season ended, I started going to the Oklahoma State wrestling room and began working out with the team. The harder I worked the happier I was.

March rolled around, and the NCAA finals were coming up. The head coach at Oklahoma State was Tommy Chesbro and his assistant was my best friend, Paul Martin. I had worked camps with Tommy and Paul, so they always welcomed me in the wrestling room.

I can still remember Coach Chesbro coming to me and asking if I would like to go to the national tournament with the team. What an honor, I couldn't pass it up.

I went to my principal, Dr. Purcell to ask for the week off so I could join the OSU team when they travelled to Princeton for the NCAA finals. His reply was a flat no.

I had locked horns with him over the job and now he was asserting his authority. I defiantly told him I was going anyway. He retorted "I'll dock your pay".

Fine with me, considering I had no idea what docking my pay was. To make a long story short, I went to the NCAA tournament, got my pay docked.

I later found out that getting your pay docked is not getting paid for the week, but they also take out $100 a day to pay for your sub. My check was awful small that month, but I could have cared less. I had the greatest time at Princeton and I had found my niche in life.

I spent a great deal of time hanging out in the coaching office with Paul and Coach Chesbro.

Have you ever been in a room and felt totally comfortable? No underlying urge to leave or that feeling you are invading someone's space. Being in the office just felt right, like I belonged there.

One spring day, Coach Chesbro was sitting behind his desk and I was by the conference table thumbing through one of the wrestling magazines.

Suddenly he breaks the silence, "Mark, why don't you come and coach with us?"

No way, he didn't just ask me to coach with him. My heart started to race, my face flushed, and this strange warm feeling invaded my whole body.

He went on to offer me a graduate assistantship. I would receive tuition money to finish my master's degree in zoology and a stipend of $210 a month.

In return I would have to teach 2 bowling classes and a methods of coaching wrestling class. At that moment I felt I had just won the lottery. A graduate assistant coach at Oklahoma State University, a dream job.

I said "wow, yes, thank you, sweet, OK". I was blubbering and so excited I could hardly contain myself. Granted I am leaving a $2200 a month job for $210 a month job, so Coach and Paul are looking at me like I am crazy for not at least thinking about it.

When a dream job is offered, pay is always the last thing on my mind. I know the money will always work itself out. Being happy, having fun, pursuing a dream that is my work ethic. I have never cared much for money, but I certainly have pursued fun in my life.

This step was one of many I have taken to pursue some very rewarding work. Resigning from my teaching job in Cushing was one of the best days I have ever had.

Being young, single, with no cares made it tough to be accountable and responsible. Dr. Purcell sure did smile when I handed in my resignation. I was always in the hot seat, late for faculty meetings, not getting my grades in on time, but mostly walking around so excited for my next opportunity.

At the end of the year I still had 10 sick days on my contract that were paid sick days. I called in sick 2 weeks in a row. I figured it was payback for docking my pay when I went to the national tournament.

We would hitch up the ski boat, head to the lake, and water ski the day away. The ironic part of going to the lake, I would pass Dr. Purcell's house on the way. I always made it a point to wave as I passed, never got a wave back, but I still chuckle remembering him shaking his head in disgust.

My first teaching assignment at Oklahoma State was 2 bowling classes. I had been bowling but had no idea how to teach bowling.

Oklahoma State had a competitive bowling team and the woman that coached the team was face to face with me. A rather large, older woman with short graying hair glaring at me, looking me up and down.

"Do you know what the 3-6-9 spare adjustment system is?" I was like a deer in the headlights, my eyes showed fear and she pounced. "I suppose you have never heard of the 3-1-2 strike adjustment either?"

She was so serious, she loved her sport and her passion was contagious. I absorbed the information and we quickly became friends.

She did teach me the systems and I listened. In the end, I probably did do decent job.

None of my students had ever seen me bowl, they all believed I knew what I was doing. At the start of each semester I would teach the 3-1-2 strike adjustment with the natural hook delivery over the 2nd arrow.

Almost every semester I taught, I would only throw 1 ball, and for some uncanny reason I would get a strike. That would be the only ball I would roll the rest of the semester.

Each class would ask me to bowl with them, I would dodge the question, stating I was going to bowl with the next class. I never did show them I couldn't bowl. Sometimes a bluff works, but in the end no matter how hard you bluff you will get discovered.

Fate unfolds itself in strange ways. My year at Oklahoma State was a dream come true. Wrestling in the afternoon and teaching during the day, all the while being on one of the most exciting campuses in America.

I was dating or at least trying to date a girl named Patty. Right before Christmas I was sat down and given the "dear John" speech. She went on to explain she had a boyfriend that had been away and now he was returning to school.

She was letting me know they were going to get together. Tough pill to swallow, but I graciously bowed out.

That January I would see the two of them together. She was a stunning blonde, high cheekbones, brown eyes, and a smile that shined.

He was a small guy, probably only 130 pounds. Somehow, he had a super tan for the middle of January. Dressed a little preppy and did seem like he enjoyed life, always had a smile or a laugh. They both looked happy together, which of course, just bewildered me.

His name was Tony Cosby. He had just returned from New Zealand. Tony was an avid rock climber and had taken a semester off to go to New Zealand and rock climb. Summertime in the southern hemisphere is our winter and Tony came back to OSU with quite a summer tan.

Our social circles intertwined occasionally, and I would catch myself staring or maybe even glaring at Tony.

One Saturday night we both were at a party, Tony walks over to me and says "why are you always staring at me? Do we know each other?"

I smile and explain that I am totally confused why Patty would blow me over for you. Just did not make any sense to me.

He started to laugh, it was a funny belly laugh from deep within. Now I am confused, Tony went on to explain Patty had given him the same 'dear John" speech I had been given.

The twist was, she wanted to quit dating Tony, so she could resume dating me. He was wondering, why Patty would blow him over for me. Our friendship and journey started that night. We became inseparable friends, neither of us ever did date Patty again.

Tony and I shared one thing, a passion for living. I had moved to the beach the summer of my junior year in college, but Tony had moved to New Zealand to follow his passion of rock climbing.

I admired his resolve to do what he wanted. One night I was thumbing through an outdoor magazine and noticed an article about whitewater rafting.

Out of the blue, I said "I would love to be a whitewater rafting guide." Granted, I had never even seen a whitewater river but still had this desire to be a guide.

The semester was wrapping up at OSU and Tony was headed to Jackson Hole, Wyoming to work as a climbing guide in the Tetons. Tony nonchalantly said, "why don't you come with me to Jackson Hole, there is a whitewater river you could guide on."

I had no plans for the summer, mulled it over for a second and said, "I'm going!"

Chapter 6

Jackson Hole

Jackson Hole, Wyoming is not the most desirable place to be the first of May. Winter is still trying to hold on and believe me, winters in Jackson Hole can be brutal.

The day we arrived, the freezing drizzle and the cloudy skies still could not withhold the beauty of Jackson Hole and the Grand Tetons. Tony had secured a room for us at a Baptist Mission house.

Randy and Ann Foster were Baptist missionaries that provided a church for the members of the Baptist faith in Jackson Hole. The mission also recruited young college age students to conduct weekend campfire devotionals around various Jackson Hole campsites.

All in all, there were around 15 young people that served and stayed at the mission just outside of Jackson Hole during the summers.

After settling in and unpacking our bikes we headed in to town. Town was 6 miles away, so a brisk ride into the town was very welcomed and needed.

Tony and I parted, he was off to see about his summer climbing school position and I was off to land a whitewater guiding position. Sounds simple enough, but for one glitch, I had no idea what a whitewater river was.

There were 5 river companies in town and as I rode my bike down Jackson Hole main street looking into the storefront windows, I could not help wondering, which one should I venture into? Some call it fate, others call it divine intervention.

I was drawn into a small 8 by 10 office tucked back and a little out of the way. On the sign it read Lewis and Clark U paddle trips.

I opened the door and behind the counter was a man, not an ordinary man, but a larger than life man. Not real muscular, but not fat, just noticeable. He removed his glasses and with the oddest grin, looked up and said “yes?”

At that moment our eyes locked, he had the most amazing eyes, they had a sparkle with a scent of mischief. I knew I wanted to work for him, I probably would have worked for free. His name was Rod Lewis and he was the sole owner of Lewis and Clark rafting.

I boldly blurted out “I want to be a whitewater river guide.” Rod looked up with a sly grin and responded, “what experience do you have?” Seemed like a fair question since most employers love experience and knowing I had none, it was time to improvise.

I explained that I had never been on a whitewater river, but if you would train me, I would run the river the exact way you want me to.

"Really, you have never been on a river and you want to be a guide?"

At that moment the office door opened and in walked Shawn. A good looking rugged young man from the east coast. Sean was an assistant alpine ski coach for the US Olympic ski team during the winter and was looking for a summer job.

He looks at Rod Lewis and says, "I want to be a whitewater river guide." Now at this moment Rod is shaking his head and says, "I suppose you have never been on a river either."

Shawn looked at me and smiled "nope, but it sure looks fun." I liked Shawn from the very first moment we met.

We both had dreams, passion, and a love for fun. Rod pauses a moment, shakes his head and says the sweetest words "I'll train you, you will start tomorrow 8 o'clock."

Shawn and I look at each other, smiles as big as Texas, realizing we just landed a dream job of a lifetime. Neither of us asked what the pay was, we both were following our passion and knew the money would take care of itself.

The next morning, we showed up to the office ready to be trained. I have my wetsuit, Shawn has his, and we load into the van.

Jackson Hole is cold the first part of May. There are still traces of snow around town. We both know the snow melt river water is going to be bone chilling cold.

Rod begins the drive out of town but turns into an automotive shop, we both wonder why. As he puts the van in park he says, "time to work."

Both Shawn and I look at each other with bewilderment, wondering what this is all about.

The three of us walk into the body shop and there before us is a yellow school bus. Rod with his wily grin, explains that after the bus is sanded for repainting he will train us on the river. He hands us the sandpaper and off he goes.

My first thought "are you kidding me!" Sanding a school bus before going to train on the river was Rod's way of checking our commitment.

Three days of sanding and the bus was ready to be painted. We both knew what Rod Lewis was doing, but both Shawn and I had a dream, so we sanded and dreamed of being on the river.

Three days later, we were headed to the river in the van, overcast with a temperature of 40 degrees, a bit nippy to be on a river.

The Snake River boat launch for the whitewater section just south of Jackson Hole is a 20-minute ride. The excitement and anticipation are hard to describe. The adrenaline rush is so exhilarating, but flat out fear is a real emotion also.

We pull into West Table boat launch, a large parking area with access to the river. Rod throws the inflatable boat out onto the ground and Shawn and I take turns operating the pump as the 17-foot Rogue inflatable raft starts to resemble a boat.

We all 3 don our wetsuits, since the water temperature is about the same as the air temperature.

Your first love, losing your virginity, and your first whitewater river are events that you will never forget.

Being on a whitewater river for the first time, surreal is the only word that comes to mind. Hearing the rapids before seeing them makes it even more exciting.

Rod is guiding from the back of the boat, Shawn and I are paddling in the front of this large raft. Going down the river Rod gives the safety talk, floating with your feet downstream, holding on to your paddle making your arm longer, and not to panic.

The river is starting to flow at flood stage which makes the rapids larger and more challenging. My heart is pounding so hard, I can feel it in my throat. Rapid after rapid we go.

Rod would point out a hole, or reversal in the river and nonchalantly say, "stay out of there, that hole will kill you."

There is an underwater shelf on the left-hand side of the Snake River. As the water flows over the shelf, the water reverses back into itself.

This rapid will flip the raft and recirculate the people around and around, much like a washing machine.

The summer prior to us being there, a woman lost her life in this rapid. Rod had performed CPR for over an hour on her.

The dangers are real, and as we floated by, seeing the power of a whitewater river is so humbling.

There is a rapid called Lunch Counter on the Snake River, the premier rapid of the 8-mile run. This rapid has 7 huge standing waves, each about a 10-foot wall of water.

As we approach the roar of the rapid is deafening, my heart pounding, Rod yelling, "Stab the wave in the throat and pull the boat through!"

Seven times Shawn and I stabbed the wave and pulled the raft through and then it was over, calm swirling water all around.

What a rush! At that moment I knew I would do anything to be a whitewater river guide.

We finished our eight-mile run. Rod walked to the highway to hitch hike back to his car and Shawn and I deflated the raft and waited for Rod to return.

As we reminisced together we both knew we would do whatever it takes to be a guide.

Once the raft was loaded into the car and we head back to the West Table boat launch. Rod casually explains after Shawn and I run the river 20 times, he will make us guides.

Back at the boat launch, I think the 3 of us are going to do the run again. Not so, Rod pulls out another boat from the back of the van, throws it on the ground, and says he will be back at 5 o'clock to pick us up. " Get as many runs in as you can".

We both look at each other as Rod drives off, whoa, we did not see that coming. As we unfold the boat, we can clearly see this is a much smaller boat than we had just went down the river in. The raft was a 9-foot Achilles inflatable raft, it looked like a mini boat.

That moment was a defining moment, Shawn and I looked at each other and we both knew we were going to die.

We had to document 20 trips with this small boat on our own. Being determined to be a whitewater river guide we launched into our first training trip.

The 9-foot Achilles raft was so much smaller, and the waves seemed so much larger. The only upside was the small raft was much easier to handle.

Neither Shawn nor I had ever been in a whitewater river up until 3 hours ago and now we are embarking on our first solo trip into the Snake River rapids together.

No clue as how to steer the raft, no clue on how to read the rapids, and no clue what to do if we flip the raft.

We see our first rapid approaching; our hearts and adrenaline are racing and wham.

We flip the raft in the very first rapid. We have our lifejackets on but we both are stunned. The water is ice water, what a wakeup call.

We are both hanging on to an overturned raft as we float down the middle of a flood staged Snake River. We look at each other, shake our heads and we both begin to laugh.

What have we done? Getting our wits back I shout "we need to be on the right side to get out" that happened to be where the road was.

We were struggling trying to swim and holding on to an overturned raft when suddenly Shawn shouted, "I think the hole that can kill you is up ahead".

I immediately let go of the raft and hightailed to the right-hand shore and so did Shawn. Both of us now safely on shore, we watch our raft continues down the river without us.

Hiking up the hill to the road we both know somehow, we must get the raft back. Hitchhiking was our only answer, to our amazement an attractive woman about our age stopped and picked us up.

We both were cold and wet, also a little freaked out about what just happened. As we explained to her what happened, it was humorous and periodically we would pull the car over and look for our raft.

The Snake River rapids cover 8 miles, we flipped within the first mile. Traveling the length of the rapids, still no sign of our raft.

The Snake River empties into Palisades Reservoir and sure enough there was our upside-down raft smack dab in the middle of Palisades Reservoir. Somehow, I drew the unlucky straw and had to swim to the raft and bring it to shore.

Not an easy swim with a lifejacket and a paddle in freezing snowmelt water. By the time we hitchhiked back the day was coming to an end, we headed back to Jackson Hole with quite a story to tell.

Shawn and I proceeded to do our 20 training trips. Flipping the raft multiple times, figuring out how to flip it back over and climb back in together.

I do believe Rod Lewis wanted us to swim the entire river and believe me; that is one way to figure out how water flows.

Looking back, that was probably the most times I have come close to death in a very short period.

Our river training was complete, now it was time to learn how to deal with passengers. Rod introduced us to John Silverman.

John had been an employee and lead boatman for the last 5 years. He was not returning but doing Rod a favor by training the 4 new guides that would become Lewis and Clark U Paddle guides.

We mingled with the passengers and watched John make his magic. Confidence, reassurance, and fun were the components we had to master before taking our first group of passengers' solo.

Soon we were all flying solo with our own boat and passengers and what a ride and rush it was.

Three trips a day down the whitewater section and then on our days off, back to the river in our kayaks. For the next 5 summers I lived in Jackson Hole and never did tire of it.

I became one of the lead boatman of Rod's company. My job was to train the new guides and like my training experience, I trained the new guides exactly how I was trained.

I have noticed in my life there are no directions how to do things. Marriage and raising children are prime examples. Our only frame of reference is how we were raised.

The same went for guiding with Lewis and Clark. I would take the new guides down the river and say, "stay out that hole, it'll kill you."

Then I would pull out the 9-foot Achilles raft and tell them to document 20 trips and come back and we'll talk.

I remember my 2 roommates Tony Cosby and Rich Mauro coming back to the house after swimming Cottonwood rapid, which is a half mile long.

They both glared at me and said, "you're trying to kill us!" I chuckled and explained, I don't know any other way, sorry.

My people skills blossomed during that time in my life. Fun, excitement, and adventure were what my life was all about.

Mark guiding on the Snake River (age 22)

Chapter 7

Career

As I start nearing the age of 30 I begin to ponder what should I do? I have 2 degrees in my pocket, I have had great adventures in Oklahoma and Jackson Hole. Now what do I do?.

The phone rings, and my collegiate wrestling coach from Utah State University is calling.

Bob Carlson, a man among men. Larger than life itself, Bob commanded attention when he entered a room. Persuasive, intent, and a bulldog when he wanted his way.

His eyes and intentions were set on me being his assistant wrestling coach at Utah State University. I was reluctant at first, being under Bob was certainly not a dream of mine.

I loved wrestling for the man, but I was totally happy being out of his control. After some convincing, I decided Utah State University would be my next career move.

My job as an assistant wrestling coach involved coaching and teaching 10 activity classes in the physical education department.

I had 2 bosses. Coach Carlson on the wrestling side and Dr. Robert Sorenson, head of the physical education department on the teaching side.

My office was in the physical education building along with the wrestling room. I taught various classes such as, golf, tennis, softball, and weight training.

Utah State University was on a quarter system and spring quarter was about to begin in. My schedule that quarter included teaching a hiking class.

I show up the first day of class and in the front row sat a woman, super tan, long brown hair with a splash of blonde highlights, and a toned, athletic body.

She smiled, I smiled, and I was in love. From the first sight, I knew I wanted this woman and I wanted her bad. After class we talked, the chemistry was there and we both knew it. I wanted to see her that night, so I asked her to dinner and hot tubbing afterward.

She agreed, but stated she was a vegetarian. I have never dated a vegetarian, but at that point I really didn't care, I knew I would figure something out.

Her name was Laurie Rucker, she not only became my girlfriend that night, but later became my wife and mother of my 2 children.

Now Laurie and I did have our dating problems. I was 6 years older, and she was finishing her undergraduate degree.

I had met Ron Campbell, the Utah State University bookstore manager, and had become friends. Ron's love for Whitewater Rivers instantly bonded us as friends. Every morning we would have coffee together before we started our day. The more we talked, the more we wanted to be on the river.

Ron and I came up with a plan. Ron had an old school bus and I owned 2 seventeen-foot inflatable rafts with all the lifejackets and paddles.

We decided to start our own river rafting company. Taking a group of 30 students, 4 weekends in April, and 3 weekends in May to Moab, Utah. We would float an 8-mile section of the Colorado River and then the next day, hike Arches National Park.

I called the park and secured free admission tickets since I was an instructor at Utah State. We prepared 2 meals for the students, gave them a guided whitewater trip and a free day in Arches National Park before returning to Logan, Utah.

Both Ron and I were able to pocket $1,000 for the weekend. Pretty sweet gig for having a great time with these kids.

Laurie's uncle Bob was a river runner from Idaho. She grew up running rivers with her dad and uncle so rafting and camping were second nature to her. She would accompany me on the Moab trips, socialize, help, and just simply enjoy the trips.

I coached and taught my classes, but I knew I wanted a little more. I started my own Utah State Wrestling Camps.

During the summer I would employ my wrestlers to put on evening camps all around the area.

I would send my wrestlers to the high schools in Utah, Wyoming, and Idaho to conduct the clinic and I would make a 1-day appearance.

My camp system started small but quickly grew into a profitable enterprise.

My biggest success story with my camp system was offering a day camp at the Utah State University and giving a football ticket with the clinic.

The year was 1984 and the football game was Utah State verses BYU. The year before BYU had just won the national championship and every one of their games were sold out.

I was offering a $20 wrestling clinic with a free USU vs. BYU football ticket. To make a long story short, 700 wrestlers showed up.

That was $14,000 I made in 1 day. Occasionally you hit a homerun in life, this was my homerun.

Once I paid all my expenses I was still able to pocket around $10,000, not bad since my teaching salary was just $20,000 for the year.

Chapter 8

Marriage

Laurie and I were in love, we spent every free moment we had together.

That spring Jeff Minor, a wrestler of mine, and myself became certified SCUBA divers. Once our certification was finished, Jeff and I planned on going to go to the California coast and dive for the month of June.

Jeff had plans to visit his sister in Hawaii and was going to fly out of Los Angeles the first of July.

We were planning to stay on the beach and live in the back of my Volkswagen van.

Now Laurie is in the picture, the three of us got along very well and I invited her to come with us. She was always up for an adventure. Three hippies ready to explore the California coast in a beat up old Volkswagen van.

This van was unique, I had made a homemade bed in the back, tied my Kayak on top and stored everything in drawers under the bed.

The van was beige colored but had rusted severely and I had painted a large yellow stripe down the side to help stop the rust.

Laurie's home was in Bountiful, Utah. Bountiful is the Mormon capital of the world. Her parents were full-fledged Mormons and I had never met them. Here I am picking their daughter up and taking her to California, I can only imagine what was going through their mind.

Pulling into the driveway both Fred and Carol Rucker are outside waiting. I smile at Jeff and say, "this is going to be good."

Questions started flying, where are you going? How long will you be gone? Where are you going to say? When will you be back? All legitimate questions that I had no answer for, just shook my shoulders and smiled.

Off to California we went. Once there we started to follow the beach volleyball circuit.

At that time the stars were Singin Smith and Randy Stokla, both pioneers of the sport. Diving, surfing, and volleyball was our life.

We would use the beach showers and bathrooms, park the van in a residential neighborhood to sleep and cook most of our meals on a beach fire.

We traveled the beaches from Santa Barbara to Ensenada, Mexico. We said goodbye to Jeff at the end of June and spent the month of July playing before returning to Utah.

When I reminisce, that was probably the best time of my life. In love, free, and enjoying every part of the day with the woman of my dreams.

Once back in Utah, Laurie and I had our ups and downs. Broke up, got back together and then we did finally marry.

We bought a house, then bought another house just 2 doors away. We moved our belongings with a shopping cart.

Had our first child, a beautiful little girl we named Whitney. Children do not come with instructions and our first night at home with Whitney was a long night.

Every hour she was crying, I asked Laurie if she was hungry, but the answer was no. We would hold her and off to sleep she would go.

The next morning, we are telling the next-door neighbor of our dilemma. The neighbor asked, "what kind of pajamas did she have?" I looked at Laurie, and she looked at me, "pajamas?"

Both Laurie and I slept naked, didn't even dawn on us that our new baby girl needed to stay warm with pajamas.

There is always a time when you realize you are a totally incompetent parent.

Chapter 9

Chasing Money

Never in my life had I ever chased money. My firm belief in pursuing fun and knowing money will always follow still holds true today.

Sometimes you fall off the wave of life and sure enough, this was one of those times.

My coaching and teaching career at Utah State University was everything I had ever wanted. Four years as an assistant wrestling coach and then two years as the head wrestling coach.

I was on top of the coaching world, always wondering what is next. March 1989 was a turning point in my life, I received the best news of my life, and the worst news, of my life.

The good news was my wife was pregnant with our second child. The bad news was Utah State University had just eliminated the wrestling program due to title 9.

With the second child on the way and half of my job eliminated was the order of the day. I pondered what to do and one option was going back to the high school level to coach and teach.

Clovis West High School in Fresno, California had heard of the wrestling program being dropped and quickly acted on recruiting me as their next coach.

I was reluctant at first to consider the job. Going back to the high school level was something I really did not want to do.

Once in Fresno, California and seeing the school system, seeing my salary, and seeing the type of home I could buy, I quickly signed my teaching contract.

Clovis West had doubled my salary, we bought a home on Woodward Lake. This was a community of homes on a man-made lake with a swimming pool, sailboats, and fully stocked lake with fish.

The highlight of my 4 years in Fresno teaching and coaching was my son Willie being born.

I have always had a wandering eye when it comes to jobs. I was attending the Madera fair not far from Fresno when I noticed the pony ride.

My daughter was now 4 years old and loved the ponies. This ride had 5 ponies walking in a circle. That day, Whitney rode each pony. She would get off one pony, immediately get in line to ride another.

While waiting I struck up a conversation with the pony ride owner and operator. I asked, “what else do you do to make a living?” I assumed the pony ride business was a side business and he had a real job somewhere.

He looked at me and smiled, "this is my job." No way, you can a living with just 5 ponies.

He had me follow him to his camper trailer, there he pulled out a scrapbook and showed me exactly what the ponies had provided for him. In my amazement was a beautiful ranch house, trucks, trailers, and land.

The next week I started buying ponies, building a ring, and designing a pony sweep. I was determined to have my own pony ride business.

Growing up in Iowa and working with pigs and riding horses in the country, this seemed to be a natural fit with the ponies.

I spent a day at the Fresno State University library researching all the fairs and festivals around the area.

The central valley of California has so many festivals, the almond festival, the peach festival, orange days, and the garlic festival.

The Fresno Bee newspaper on Thursday always mentioned the fairs and festivals for the weekend. An organizer phone number was always listed, and this was gold in my pocket.

The first year I was in business I was making $1,000 a day, often I would have to pin a sign on a little girl's back saying, do not line up behind me the ponies are tired.

The lines would go on and on. The longer the line, the shorter the pony ride and I do believe that was fine with the parents that had been standing in the long line.

I mentioned earlier about falling off the wave of life. Teaching at Clovis West High School was falling off that wave.

After my third year of coaching I was fired from the wrestling position. However, I retained my teaching position because I had earned tenure in the California system.

I had never failed, this was virgin territory for me. The wrestling program was not having the success that they thought I would bring to the program.

Looking back, hindsight is always 20-20. I did spend too much time with my 2 young children. I really couldn't help it, I was madly in love with both of my children.

The time spent with the ponies was a diversion, I thought a healthy diversion but, it did impede on my coaching responsibilities.

I once was the favorite child of the Clovis West kingdom and now I quickly became a liability.

The administration was now gunning to fire me from my teaching position and the knit picking began.

When I did finally give the administration my resignation letter, my female administrator said, "Now I don't have to come after you anymore, thank you."

I knew she was ordered to get me out of the system, and I knew it was hard on her to ride me that hard about everything. I liked her, and I know deep down she liked me, but the competitive system Clovis schools had in place was starting to unravel.

When one door closes, another door always opens. We sold our house, made quite a bit of money and the extra money from the ponies meant we had a cushion to figure out our next move.

Chapter 10

Back to Utah

Moving back to Utah was a new adventure. My father-in-law offered us a business opportunity that sounded quite different.

He and his wife decided they would go on a 2-year Mormon mission and turn the car wash business over to my wife and me. Running a car wash business was foreign to me, but what the heck, a new adventure.

My in-laws led a modest lifestyle, so I was not sure exactly how much a car wash business could make.

Once again, I jumped in thinking this might be fun without knowing the earning potential.

Riding this wave was very lucrative. One evening my wife and I were counting the week's money and I said to her, "did you know your parents made this kind of money?"

She had no idea, and neither did I, that the car wash business would way surpass a teaching salary.

We purchased a home, not an ordinary home but a geodesic dome house. This house is round and built with triangles.

Supposedly dome houses are built to survive earthquakes, but in all honesty, they are a strange looking house.

The home was situated on horse property, which was ideal for my ponies. Often, I would go to the livestock auction and buy goats, sheep, calves, and horses.

I would feed them and keep them around until the kids tired of them and then back to the auction they went.

One time I brought home a pregnant nanny goat. I thought it would be fun for the kids to see a newborn baby goat. She did deliver, but only 1 baby came out.

Most goats deliver twins, so I knew I would have to palpate her to see if the second baby was stuck or make sure her womb was barren.

She was a small goat; my hand was too large. I call my wife over and explain the situation and ask her to palpate the goat.

Convincing her to lube up her arm and go inside the goat was no easy task, but my wife was an animal lover and she did palpate her first and last goat.

Chapter 11

Rodeo Cowboy

As with most couples the years go by, the kids are growing up, first day at school, summer vacations, and soon you are caught up into the web of life.

Running a business, being a dad, trying to be a good husband, was pretty much the routine.

My college friend Scott Tillotson had purchased a guest ranch in Wise River, Montana. The kids and I enjoyed going to the ranch, horseback riding, four wheeling, and fishing on the river that ran through this gorgeous property.

If there is a heaven, this ranch would be the closest thing to heaven I have ever been. One afternoon as Scott and I sat on the porch contemplating life, we both looked out on the 200 acres of pasture and decided we should buy a herd of longhorn cattle.

Was there money to be made raising longhorn cattle? The answer is a firm no. We did both jump in and soon we were the proud owners of a small longhorn cattle herd.

This small herd gave us an excuse to head to Montana. We would load up the truck, I would take my young son, Willie. Scott would usually take his 2 youngest daughters, Summer and Jackie.

Off to Montana we would go, using the cows as an excuse to enjoy the clean sweet air of Montana.

Every spring we would have a new calf crop. The calves needed to be vaccinated and the male calves had to be castrated.

Scott owned fox trotter horses. These horses are designed to cover a lot of ground in a short amount of time with extreme comfort. These horses are a dream to ride, but as working cow horses, that is entirely a whole different story.

The horses didn't like the ropes being swung, they really didn't like the cows at all. These horses were bred to travel not doctor cattle. One winter evening Scott called and asked if I wanted to go team roping with him.

Team roping is a rodeo sport where there is a steer, usually around 400 pounds loaded into a chute.

Two cowboys are involved, the header and the healer. On the left side of the chute is the header. He is the cowboy that ropes the horns of the steer and turns the cow to the left.

The healer starts from the right side of the chute and comes in behind and ropes the 2 back feet of the steer. This is called team roping, this is a timed event.

Once the steer is roped, head and feet, the flag drops and the 2 cowboys who can do this the fastest are the winners of the rodeo.

Scott's neighbors were team ropers and had invited him to come to a practice arena and try it.

We loaded up our fox trotter horses and off we went to the Blue Sky Arena. We were team roping for the very first time.

Some waves in life are modest, some waves are wild. This wave of life was quite a ride.

We both saddled up our horses, the nerves were starting to set in. The adrenaline is flowing as both Scott and I load our horses into the roping chute.

The chute opens and off to the races we go. The steer is on a full sprint, we are racing after the steer.

Scott flings his rope, our horses not sure what we are doing. We didn't have a chance in hell of catching that steer, but from that moment, Scott and I are totally hooked on team roping.

What an adrenaline rush. Team roping is mass chaos for 8 seconds and then it is all over. There are 5 variables in one scenario. A 400-pound steer, two 1,000-pound horses and 2 cowboys with lariats trying to capture an animal that does not want to be captured.

Many things can and do go wrong, but the thrill and the adrenaline rush are second to none, and at that moment I was hooked.

I came home that night and told my wife "I am going to be a professional rodeo cowboy."

Looking back in hindsight, I should have broken that news in pieces rather than all at once.

We watched videos on how to team rope, read articles, and we both bought roping horses.

What made us successful in the beginning was buying horses that knew more about the sport than we did. Our horses always put us into position and all we had to do was throw the rope and catch.

Our lives revolved around roping. Practicing 2 nights a week, competing on the weekends soon was our way of life. My business only needed me there for 2 hours out of the day and Scott was into multi-level marketing which gave him a lot of free time.

Being a rodeo cowboy is a little crazy. Once you win a rodeo, you always take your winnings and enter more rodeos.

At the end of rodeo season, you have a mad wife and a worn-out truck. Was it worth it? The answer is a firm yes, what a ride.

I will never forget the first rodeo I won.

My team roping partner was Joel Ivie, a true rodeo cowboy. We had entered the Castle Dale, Utah rodeo.

Joel and I entered the roping arena, since Joel was a local the crowd cheered. My heart is racing, the chute opens, off we go.

Joel ropes the horns and turns the steer, I dive behind the steer and throw my rope. I pull the rope taut and 2 feet are in the rope.

Wow, what a feeling, our time was under 6 seconds and I know we have just won the team roping event.

My hat falls off and I drop my rope. I am so excited I jump off my horse and look into the crowd. I see my 10-year-old daughter Whitney.

Her arms are raised high, cheering with the crowd. This is a moment in time, when time stops.

I am soaking in this sweet moment when I hear the rodeo announcer "if this cowboy would ever get his gear and get out of the arena we could continue."

The crowd laughed, I collected my and hat and rope, even had to chase down my horse. Whitney is just as excited as I was to win the rodeo.

That evening at the rodeo dance, my daughter asked, "Daddy will you dance with me?" Holding my daughter and dancing to the Anne Murray song "Could I have this dance for the rest of my life" will be a moment I will treasure the rest of my life.

As I write the words, tears well up just remembering that special moment.

I did do well that season, won a saddle, some buckles and a few more rodeos. Riding this wave was a fun wave to catch, I call this the rodeo wave.

Team roping (I'm on the left age 38)

I won this saddle in 1997 (age 40)

Chapter 12

The Big "D"

Relationships are defined by growing together as a couple or growing apart as a couple. Never does a relationship remain the same.

My marriage to Laurie was slowly over time growing apart. She had her friends, I had my friends and very often we had separate lives but lived in the same house.

Looking back, my fascination with Montana and the rodeo lifestyle was not her dream. Both were my dreams and I pursued them with energy and vigor.

Laurie and I tried to figure life out but, in the end, we knew the marriage was over. As I loaded up my things into the truck, hitched the horse trailer up and started to drive away my 8-year-old son Willie became my hero.

I was about 2 miles down the road when he called me and begged me to come back and get him. I turned around and at that moment I knew Willie was my life.

Willie never left my side growing up, we ate together, played football, basketball, and baseball constantly. When an 8-year-old child gives you his heart unconditionally, he becomes your hero. Willie was and still is a tremendous athlete.

Occasionally you do something right as a parent. I never missed a football game of Willie's. Somehow I made it to every game he played .

He started playing when he was 6 years old, and went on to play college football at Weber State University. Watching Willie play at Boston College, Texas Tech, BYU and other major places was certainly a treat for me. I am a very proud parent of 2 outstanding children.

Laurie and I divorced as friends, our 2 children adjusted, and we still today remain, friends.

Divorce is a wave that is hard to fall off of. Time heals, and life does go on, but saying goodbye to someone you love is falling off the wave of life.

After the divorce, I ended up with 2 of the 4 car washes. Being a newly single guy being tied down to a business wasn't very appealing and I began searching for my next wave to climb back onto.

My college roommate had just taken the head football coaching job in Layton, Utah where I had my home. After his first year, Steve Smith mentioned there was a Biology teaching position opening at Layton High school.

He also was wondering if I would like to coach with him. As I pondered the move, it seemed like quite the opportunity.

Once again, I got back on another wave of life. I returned the car washes back to my in-laws and started my teaching and coaching career at Layton High School in Layton, Utah.

Chapter 13

Research Scientist

Teaching high school Biology and coaching football quickly became my life. I was really enjoying raising Willie and watching him mature as an athlete.

We were the epitome of being bachelors. The laundry room was both of our closets. I had 2 shelves and Willie had 2 shelves. We both dressed and undressed in the laundry room, our clothes never did see our bedrooms.

As a Biology teacher I started to notice different opportunities show up in my emails. In the science field there was a big push for research scientists to include teachers in their research so their work would get out into the public domain.

The Armada Project, NOAA Teacher at Sea, and Earthwatch all had research opportunities to apply for. I thought, what the heck I'll throw my name in the hat.

As fate would have it, or I like to think of as the next wave starting to build, I started to get chosen for various scientific expeditions.

My first expedition was estimating whale and dolphin populations in the tropical Pacific.

I then was offered a chance to tag Crabeater seals in Antarctica.

I tagged sea turtles in Uruguay and Mexico and even counted tropical birds in Costa Rica.

The wild part of this was, they were paying me to do this. All of my travel and expenses plus they were giving me a stipend on top of my teaching salary.

Writing the grants was like a competition for me. I would celebrate with the victories and wonder what happened when I wasn't chosen.

An up and down ride, but that is what getting on the wave of life feels like.

When I met my second wife to be (it's never a good idea to number your wives), Stacey was a pre-kindergarten teacher in Park City, Utah.

We had a mutual friend that decided we would make a great couple. Our friend mentioned to me that Stacey was a former Miss Arizona and fourth runner-up in the 1976 Miss America beauty pageant.

With the help of google I learned a little about Stacey even before our date had started. We did like each other's company, as we talked into the night I mentioned how I was applying for various scientific grants.

Stacey was intrigued and asked if she could apply. I figured she was a teacher and it certainly made sense for her to apply so I gave her the links for the applications.

I had just sent my application in to study Hawksbill sea turtles in Barbados, she expressed interest and said, "wouldn't it be fun if we both got the chance to go to Barbados?"

We began dating and after 4 weeks have passed since our initial first date I receive a phone call from Stacey.

"Mark, guess what! I just received a phone call from Earthwatch and I am going to Barbados to study Hawksbill sea turtles! Did you get a call?"

I was pretty stunned at this point. I sheepishly said no I haven't heard from them.

I am now in a dilemma; how can I be happy for her when I really wanted to go. On top of that, I was the one that encouraged her to apply, and she took my expedition.

My poor head was trying to come up with the words she wanted to hear. Eventually I swallowed my pride and did rejoice with her in the good news.

I knew there was only 1 position for that expedition and she was going. The more I thought about it, the more I wondered why they passed me over and took her.

After about a week I finally broke and called the Earthwatch headquarters. I explained who I was and then blurted out, "I'm not sure why I am calling, maybe just therapy but I am having a hard time being excited for my girlfriend going to Barbados to study turtles and I am staying at home. Guess I was wondering why I got left behind?"

The woman on the other end of the phone started to laugh and replied, “relax cowboy, I noticed on your application you were scuba certified and I assigned you to measure coral reefs in Jamaica, I will send your letter tomorrow.”

Oh wow, those words were so sweet to hear. The past week I had felt like Charlie Brown with the cloud hanging over his head.

Even though I thought I had fallen off the wave, another opportunity was right behind the lost one.

Measuring coral reefs in Jamaica (age 48)

Stacey and I married in April. She spent the month of June in Barbados working with Hawksbill sea turtles. I spent the month of July in Jamaica measuring coral reefs.

Our love grew, common interests, travel and we both loved teaching.

The surfing community is a close-knit group. They watch out for each other, protect each other, and inform each other.

Shortly after Stacey and I returned to normal life after our summer expeditions she decided to host a movie night party at our house, inviting her Park City, Utah friends. My house was a 50-minute drive from Park City so there was going to be travel time involved.

During her Park City days, she and her friends would get together every Monday night to have a pot luck dinner and enjoy a movie together.

Stacey was so excited to host movie night at our house. She invited the group of 12 regulars and some part timers.

She had the house looking immaculate and was ready to show off her new life with me. The food was all laid out, the movie was rented, and the party was ready to begin.

One hour before the party was to start, Stacey received a phone call from one of the expected guests.

She was informed her best friend decided to change movie night to her house in Park City and left Stacey with no one showing up.

Every guest went to movie night in Park City and left Stacey and I all alone.

I have experienced disappointment and heart ache but to see Stacey start to cry was a lot for me to handle. Betrayal by your best friend is a double-edged sword. Not only did she lose her Park City friends, she lost her best friend.

To this day, when I am invited to a party I always show up no matter what. During our short marriage Stacey was thrown a lot of curves. Some she handled with grace, others just plain blew up.

A second marriage is never easy especially when children are involved. I had 2 children and Stacey had 2 children from our first marriages. My son was 16 years old and for the last 8 years he and I had been living as bachelors together.

We had a system for laundry, a system for meal time, and a system for play time. A new woman in the mix was not welcomed, and I was in the middle.

Over time our relationship suffered, and we divorced just short of 2 years being married.

The wave of being married to Stacey was one of the sweetest waves I have ever caught. The fun we had and the love we shared was so memorable.

Falling off that wave was like surfing a dangerous reef. Knowing the wave is going to be spectacular, but the risk of falling onto the reef, is the risk you take. I took the risk, but the fall was brutal. Divorcing Stacey and losing her, was by far one of the darkest moments of my life.

Chapter 14

Cruise Ship Lecturer

I have noticed throughout this life, people come into your life for a time and then they disappear.

Life still goes on, much like the waves keep coming. Looking back at my short marriage to Stacey, she was instrumental in my path to becoming a Cruise Ship Naturalist.

Stacey and her mother enjoyed cruising. I had never been on a ship, so I had no clue what cruising was all about. Stacey was always hinting that we should go on a cruise.

Being the diligent husband, I began checking into cruises and prices. I loved everything about the destinations, the only thing I didn't like was the cost of the cruise.

I started thinking, is there a way to get my cruise comped? I love speaking in front of crowds, the cruising sounds fun, is there a way?

I decided to write to the various cruise ship companies. I sent letters to Royal Caribbean, Norwegian, Celebrity, and Princess cruises.

I introduced myself and said I would gladly share what I do in the science field if you will comp our cruise.

Guess what? Royal Caribbean said sure, how does a Caribbean cruise sound over Thanksgiving? Are you kidding me? I couldn't believe it worked.

All four companies were asking me to lecture on their ships. I was able to pick where we would like to go. If we did a back to back cruise, the company would pay my airfare.

Stacey and I were able to travel to the Amazon River, the Mediterranean, and Bermuda all for free.

Exploring the Amazon River (age 50)

Lecturing on the way to Hawaii

Chapter 15

Opportunities

I began vigorously applying for any expedition that was offered. The science community is a small interconnected community.

When the scientists discovered I didn't get seasick and I could play well with others the offers started pouring in. Between lecturing on cruise ships and the science opportunities, I was a busy boy.

Tagging Crabeater seals in Antarctica (age 53)

Tracking tropical birds in Costa Rica (age 54)

Catching and tagging sea turtles (age 54)

Chapter 16

Cruise Ship Naturalist

I rode the wave of research opportunities, cruise ship lecturing around the world, and my teaching career.

Always remember, the wave always changes, and change was about to happen. I received a phone call from Princess Cruises enrichment department.

This was a typical fall day, October 1. 2011, the leaves were turning, and winter was on it's way to Utah.

Princess Cruises asked if I would be interested in a paid position as a Naturalist to Hawaii. The contract was from October 6 to December 20, 2011.

My first question was "what is a Naturalist?" They explained the job, it seemed pretty much like what I was already doing on the cruise ships. The only glaring difference was, as a Naturalist I would be doing commentary from the ship's navigational bridge.

We discussed salary, the money was ok, but of course the salary was below what I was making as a seasoned teacher. I was at the end of my career teaching which meant I was maxed out on the sliding salary scale.

A teacher is paid extra for education and years of experience. I had 2 master's degrees and over 15 years of teaching experience which put me at the top range of what an educator could make.

I wondered about job security, so I asked, "after December 20th is there going to be more work and other contracts?"

Their reply was, "if you are good there will be more work, if you are not any good there will be no work after the contract."

Wow, that seemed blunt, but the honesty was impressive to me. I asked for a few hours to ponder the offer and they gave me 3 hours to consider before they offered their next choice.

I was torn, do I give up my retirement years? Do I give up my benefits? Do I give up my tenured salary?

Any one of those would have been a legitimate reason to tell Princess Cruises no. The new wave that was coming at me. This could be a life changing wave.

I called back and said, "I'm in, send me the contract!"

I turned in my teaching resignation the next day and 5 days later I was flying to San Francisco to start my Hawaiian contract.

My first contract was challenging. I had been working as a guest lecturer for a comped cruise and was always put up into a passenger cabin.

As a Naturalist I was assigned a crew cabin, something quite different than a passenger cabin. Having to sleep on a bunk bed with no windows in the cabin was an adjustment. I adapted and started feeling comfortable in my new position.

The Hawaii contract was a success, the audiences were extremely receptive. All in all, I left the Star Princess ship feeling like I have found my niche.

I was on the wave and the wave looked promising.

A few weeks later Princess called and asked if I would be interested in doing an Alaskan season on the Diamond Princess.

I quickly explained I had never been to Alaska. Their response was priceless, "You will figure it out."

Chapter 15

Snowbasin

Between my Hawaii and Alaska seasons I have about 4 months of free time. Wondering and brainstorming on what I should do to fill the time.

Both of my children are grown and on their own. As an empty nester I was thinking I should do something really fun.

My home in northern Utah is a short 20 minute drive to one of the most prestigious ski resorts in North America.

Snowbasin was a host of the 2002 winter Olympics. The men's and women's downhill, super G, and combined were held at Snowbasin.

A challenging but extremely fun place to ski. Both of my children learned to ski there and I spent many weekends on the mountain.

Since I was being paid to cruise the world, why not get paid to ski during my off time. I contacted guest services and inquired if the was a job showing guests around the mountain.

While I was still on the cruise ship coming back from Hawaii I was put into contact with the guest services supervisor.

We talked and before I even returned home, I had a job at the Snowbasin ski resort as a guest service host.

Another wave of life was starting form. Catching this wave looked promising, but always remember, the wave never does last.

I worked 6 days a week and truly loved every second working at Snowbasin. Greeting customers, answering questions, helping, and saying goodbye at the end of the day was my job.

After an few seasons I ran an idea to my supervisor. I said "do you think we should offer free mountain tours to first time visitors?"

He pondered it for a minute and replied "why not, sounds pretty fun."

That season we started doing a free 10 o'clock and 1 o'clock mountain tour. With anything new, the turn out was slow. Usually 2 or 3 couples would show up for the tour. Slowly the numbers started to build.

I enjoyed the time with the guests, riding the gondola and hearing their story was always a highlight for me. We would do 3 runs together and I would say good bye.

Most of the time the couples would tip me $20 and off they would go. This was a pretty good gig since I was only being paid $10 an hour.

This ski resort wave was starting to crest. When a wave crests, it is not long before you fall off.

Even though I never shared how much tip money I was making, people around start to notice. The ski school instructors started to take note of the numbers I was showing around the mountain. They started doing the math.

The straw that broke the camel's back happened on a sunny blue bird day. Three buses of a ski group arrived. This group was a 70's and older ski group that traveled the west skiing different resorts.

On the 10 o'clock tour there were 82 seniors ready for the free tour. I smiled and began our 3 run tour. We did look like a torchlight parade going down the mountain and I was the lead duck.

Well, you can imagine how much tip money I generated that day. One woman alone tipped me $100 for helping her take off her boots and carry her skis to the bus.

After that day, the ski school department head went directly to the resort general manager and demanded the touring operations be handed over to the ski school.

The program I had built from the ground up was suddenly snatched away and there was not one thing I could do about it.

The wave crested and I fell off. Riding that wave for 6 years was fun and memorable wave. I didn't return to Snowbasin after that season. I started to do my vacation time in Coronado, California.

75th
snowbasin

Chapter 16

Alaska

Joining my first ship in Whittier, Alaska was an eye-opening experience.

I flew into the Anchorage airport around the first of May and boarded the bus to the ship. The port Princess uses in Alaska is in Whittier, which is 65 miles from Anchorage.

The weather in the springtime of Alaska can be challenging. The wind was howling at 50 mph and it was snowing sideways.

At that moment, having never been to Alaska, my thoughts went directly to," Mark, what were you thinking?"

As I boarded the ship, I noticed the 6-inch icicles hanging on the rails. Struggling with 2 large suitcases and getting lost trying to find my new cabin, but eventually settling in.

I tried to look around, but the clouds had socked in and there was no view of any apparent Alaska beauty that I had heard so much about.

The adventure had started, and the wave was challenging, but at the same time very promising.

I did start to figure Alaska out, but I certainly didn't do it alone.

The first day on the ship the shore excursion manager named Susan came to me and asked, "how many times have you been to Alaska?" My honest answer was an embarrassing, "none."

She shook her head and replied, "I'll take care of that, you will go on the excursions I give you and then you will help me sell them."

From that moment, Susan and I became lifelong friends. She would arrange 2 excursions at every port. One excursion in the morning and another in the afternoon.

I was in Helicopters, float planes, rafts, trains, and on horses. I learned very quickly about Alaska and what the ship offered passengers.

There was a learning curve that I experienced my first year in Alaska. Speaking from the navigational bridge was one curve I had to conquer.

One voyage that was truly a memorable experience was Snow Pass. Going through Snow Pass is almost magical every time we entered the passage.

This pass is between Ketchikan and Juneau, Alaska. This is an extremely narrow passage and often filled with humpback whales feeding. Since the pass being so narrow it always brought the whales right next to the ship as we sailed through.

Humpback whales are filter feeders, meaning they do not have teeth. They have baleen plates in their mouths. They resemble long fingernail like plates, some being 8 feet long.

A humpback whales throat is no bigger than a basketball, so they don't eat large fish or marine mammals.

Their diet is krill, a small shrimplike organism. They also love small oily bait fish such as herring, capelin and sand lance. A humpback whale has throat grooves or ventral pleats that allow them to take in massive amounts of water and prey.

Once the mouth begins to close they take their 2,000-pound tongue and press it to the roof of their mouth and the water filters out between the baleen plates and they swallow their prey.

Humpback whales are noted for a behavior called "bubble net feeding". This behavior is when a group of whales, called an association, begins their hunt for food.

The association can consist of 4 to 15 whales, they are led by the dominant female of the group.

When prey is spotted the whales position themselves under the bait ball and one whale begins blowing bubbles in a perfect concentric circle around the prey.

The bubbles confuse the small fish. The group of whales come to the surface, mouths wide open and try to consume the entire school of bait fish.

I have observed humpback whales bubble net feeding in Alaska, Antarctica, Cape Cod and San Francisco. I am always amazed at the cooperation and the precision of the operation.

As we approached Snow Pass I noticed in my binoculars a large group of seabirds circling in the pass.

As I looked, I noticed the whales lunging up and consuming the fish. At that moment I knew the passengers were in for a once in a lifetime treat. I was excited beyond words.

I am positioned on the navigational bridge of the ship which has a glass like balcony that extends over the side of the ship.

This is where the captain positions himself when docking the ship.

As we approach the excitement in my voice is notable and the passengers are quickly gathering to see what is ahead.

I am almost shouting on the microphone "folks get to the port side of the ship, left hand side, hurry hurry!"

I look down and directly underneath me is a perfect circle of bubbles. In a magical moment 7 whales, mouths wide open, fish jumping, birds flying, the whales come up and feed.

Time seemed to stop, looking into the throats of 7 whales is just plain magical.

In my excitement while on the microphone I exclaim "Folks, you will never, ever see something that spectacular on any whale watching excursion!"

Much to my dismay, all the passengers went down to the shore excursion office and cancelled their whale watching excursion scheduled for the next day.

Susan the shore excursion manager was furious with me. I was called into the office of the hotel general manager and reprimanded.

It did take a few months for Susan to forgive me. She did forgive me, and now we laugh at the beginning of my Alaska career.

Chapter 17

Cruise ship life

Riding the wave of being a cruise ship naturalist has been the most exciting wave of my life. Season after season, the rewards are beyond comprehension, however in the beginning there were challenges to overcome.

The largest challenge was fitting in. We as humans are programmed to belong.

We are social animals and being accepted into a group is so satisfying and rewarding.

Being a naturalist, I am paid as an independent contractor so technically I am not part of the crew.

Since I am an employee, I am not really a passenger either. I am in this no man's land when it comes to finding my place on the ship.

When I first started his job I almost threw the towel in after the first contract.

Not belonging was tough on me, but I found there were other's in my same situation. I befriended the piano bar musician, the guest soprano, and many of the headline entertainers.

They were all in the same position as I was, and finding my clique was a welcome relief.

The joy I get when I show a passenger a whale for the first time or showing a crew member a hike they never would have discovered is unmeasurable. Their excitement is so contagious it makes me feel like I am seeing that same whale for my very first time.

When I first started this job my 5-year-old grandson called and during our conversation he asked, “grandpa is there any toys on the boat?”

I replied to Kayden, “no, I haven’t seen any toys on the boat.” Kayden went silent for a minute and then in a serious and concerned tone said” oh grandpa, how are ever going to have any fun?”

Well, I pondered that and decided, I need some toys to help me enjoy my experience on the ship.

I bought a fold up bike that I keep in my room. I also decided I need a stand-up inflatable paddle board to enjoy on the beaches of Hawaii.

I use the paddle board to reach the glaciers in Alaska that are only accessible by water.

The problem with having a bike and an inflatable paddle board is getting them on the ship.

The bike takes up a suitcase and the paddle board is another suitcase. This leaves me with only a carry on for my clothes.

When I join the ship, I have very few clothes, so in each port I buy new clothes.

I wear the new clothes every day for the next 5 months and by the end of the contract, I never want to see those clothes again.

When I leave the ship, I am happy to leave my clothes behind.

Paddling to the Mendenhall Glacier in Juneau, Alaska

My folding bike

Living in an 8 by 12-foot room for 8 months out of a year is probably not a dream situation for most people. But it sure does work for me.

I love all my meals, they are always hot and delicious. I never have to wash a dish and even my laundry is done for me. Did I mention my bed is made for me everyday and even my bathroom is cleaned daily? Does it get any better than that!

Riding this wave of being a cruise ship naturalist has been the sweetest ride of my life!!!